Yes I did that... but now I know what's

B. E. S. T.

Inc.

A collection of real life scenarios and practical guide for people serving today's youth.

By **B.E.S.T., Inc.**

ISBN: 0-9821042-0-0
ISBN-13: 9780982104200

Visit www.booksurge.com to order additional copies.

Introduction

It takes a village to raise a child is a well-known African proverb that has been used around the world for ages. When coming together to complete this book we as educators agreed with this quote but added the question: But have you seen who's running the village? We all recognize that raising children is a community effort and that we are all the sum total of our life experiences. However, we chose to examine how the baggage carried by the "elders" of the village can be detrimental and even toxic to our youth.

The content of this book is a written record of the reflections of five educators. These are not opinions but rather the voice of educators who represent over fifty years of experience as teachers, coaches, administrators, and parents who have experience with children from birth through adulthood, primarily in urban America.

B.E.S.T. Inc. is an acronym for Building Exceptional Students Together. We are comprised of experienced, certified educators and administrators with over 60 years of experience among us. Our mission is to provide exceptional educational services to those working with today's youth so that these youth will reach their full potential. Our experiences are found on all levels of education from early childhood to post college

As we have dedicated our lives to building exceptional students together by demanding excellence in all that we do, we find that our greatest lessons are not in our successes but rather in our failures. Our greatest moments of growth are born from the mistakes that we have made. This book seeks to demonstrate those mistakes, the lessons learned from those mistakes as well as the root of where our decision-making processes come from. We also offer strategies to help others who find themselves making some of the same or very similar mistakes.

When we began considering topics for our book we thought it critical to first tell our own personal stories. Stories of how we were influenced by the leaders of our villages. We looked at how our parents, educators, peers, and communities led us into becoming educators. We then looked at how these experiences shaped the type of educators we are and why we make some of the decisions we make on a daily basis. We then examined our levels of toxicity and how toxicity affected split-second decisions we made daily in the school setting.

We took a deep, introspective look at our most critical mistakes. We analyzed and documented the lessons we learned from those mistakes and offer tips for others who find they are making common mistakes or who want to take the proactive approach of avoiding the same mistakes. Let's face it. We are all human and are bound to make mistakes at some point. However, we seek to avoid making mistakes that may negatively impact the children we work with. We know that our interactions with the youth we come in contact with on a daily basis will leave a lasting impression. We seek to help others make those interactions positive ones that will bring the full potential of the youth we interact with to the forefront.

___Experiences shape our beliefs, and___
___our beliefs define our actions.___

If we want to motivate today's youth to be the best that they can be we must be the best. We become the best by sharing strategies and tips that worked for us and the things that did not work for us. We must read and attend classes and conferences on subjects that focus on our youth. We must not be afraid to say we need help and be willing to accept that help no matter what our experience level is. We are sharing our personal stories with the hope that you will learn a little more about us and tell your story.

———

Story #1

My children and I stopped at one of my favorite seafood take-out spots a few weeks ago. I have been back in my hometown for over a year now and there are moments like this when it feels so comforting. No matter how many wonderful places I visit, I swear we still have the best fried shrimp anywhere!

As we passed through the doors I saw a familiar face. "Hello, Jennifer, how are you, honey?"

"Hi, Ms. Ford! Wow, it is great to see you."

I was then introduced to a young lady who was accompanying her as a student from her first class! She said it with recognizable pride and a twinkle in her eye. After a few moments of conversation and reminiscing, we

talked about how the principal from her school was now transferring to the school where I was currently teaching.

Amazing, I thought. I have reached the point in my life where I stand side by side with the teacher who has had the most profound effect on my life. I am both proud and flabbergasted that she and I are now colleagues. I am seeking every day to impact children on the same level she impacted my life.

When I entered the third grade I was seven years old and did not know what to expect. The summer had been a rough one full of confrontations with a girl named Tiffany at the YMCA summer program. She and her friends harassed me and every day was a battle. I often got into fistfights defending myself from her verbal attacks and taunts. She and her friends called me a "stupid white girl" and once pushed and locked me into a closet. "I don't understand why." "Why does she hate me?" "Why does she keep calling me a white girl?" "I keep thinking my mother is white, not me!" "I'm only half white; why is this such a big deal?" "What is the problem?" I could not for the life of me understand what I had done to her and why I deserved to be treated like this. Imagine how my heart sank when I entered my classroom on the first day to find that Tiffany was, you guessed it, in my class!

Tiffany decided to let my first few weeks of school appear easy, but soon she eased back into her bully role in the lunchroom and on the playground. After a few weeks of this Ms. Ford handled it in our class meeting.

Mrs. Ford said, "Jennifer is BLACK and anyone who has a problem with that come see me!"

I will never forget the feeling I had at that moment. I was shocked! She had daily discussions on African-American history and the history of slavery and the status of African-Americans and biracial and multiracial people throughout history. As she spoke she was instilling a sense of self that I still have today and am grateful for.

Never had a teacher openly handled a situation that I was involved in with another student. But, I learned that was Ms. Ford's way. See, in her class we were a family. She wanted to see us treat one another as brothers and sisters should and in our family meetings we were to deal with any situations we were facing amongst ourselves.

Tiffany was not going to back down so easily though; it took months of conversations between Tiffany and Ms. Ford, Ms. Ford and myself, as well as among the three of us. However, Ms. Ford was determined to make it known that I was a part of a family and that I was safe and protected in that environment. For the first time, I had a stronger sense of self and I have never lost that. In fact, I firmly believe that it is what has helped to shape me into the confident woman I am today. More importantly, I realize that she shaped the type of relationships I have with my students. I often find myself "bullying the bullies" that I come in contact with in school settings. I am not always proud of how I handle the situations. I believe that it is my duty to protect my students. I have learned to work along

with the bullies and along with the bullied; however, I must admit, I think that my experiences in Ms. Ford's class gave me an, "Oh, NO, I'm not having that! Not in my classroom" attitude when it comes to bullying in any form!

THANK YOU, MS. FORD!

———

Story #2

My life has been influenced by so many teachers that it is difficult for me to say which one of them had the greatest impact on my life. I have been in the presence of many effective teachers, some trained and some not, but they all had the ability to share their knowledge in ways others could understand. A very limited number of them had the gift of presenting information in a very enthusiastic way while enforcing discipline with love and sensitivity. All of my teachers from first grade to fifth grade were women, strong women, who I watched and admired for their poise and ambition. They were different from my mom and I wanted to be just like them. They reminded me of the women who I admired most in my family, my aunts. They appeared to be very independent and in control of their surroundings. They were the reason I really enjoyed school. You see, school was a safe haven for me. At school, teachers encouraged me and seemed to be interested in me. My teachers, unlike my mother, wanted to hear about my ideas and activities. Yelling or focusing on your faults or imperfections was not part of their character. They corrected me with calm, firm voices and sharp eyes.

At home, I felt that my mother often misunderstood me. In some ways, I felt resented because I wanted to do things that my mother felt created financial burdens. For example, I was active at the local recreation center and no matter what I did my mother always seemed to question my intentions. I cannot remember her ever celebrating the news of my plans to be in an upcoming talent show or dance group. My dad, on the other hand, was ecstatic when I shared news with him about the activities that I was involved in at the recreation center and at school. Despite my father's feelings of intimidation, due to his lack of education, he attended major school events to show that he supported me. In fact, my time spent with my dad and his family had a profound effect on my life because of the kind words and actions they expressed toward me. They, like the teachers at school, focused on the positive attributes that I possessed.

My father's two sisters have touched my life in countless ways. My aunties showed me many things I could do in life by taking me on vacations to wonderful places and sharing their knowledge of our amazing heritage. For example, in the summer of 1983, we traveled to Georgia to visit family members and Florida to experience the wonderful adventures of Disney World's newly opened Epcot Center. They also instilled in me the importance of family traditions. For example, my family, like many African-American families,

faithfully shared Sunday dinners; my grandfather lovingly prepared ours. In fact, many of my most memorable times with my family occurred during our regular Sunday dinners at my grandparents' home, dinners that were often filled with nostalgic aromas and contagious laughter. As a child, I spent most of my summers and weekends in the suburbs in a home my grandfather built that was surrounded by trees, a flower bed, and a vegetable garden.

I later understood, after many years of frustration, that the reason my mom was so hesitant to push me to reach for my dreams was because of her upbringing. I truly believe that she did not want to see me hurt when my dreams were not fulfilled. You see, she had a dream of becoming a writer, but things happened to discourage her. My mother was the eldest of seven children who were raised by their hardworking mother alone because their father was presumed dead at an early age. Despite having very little money, my mother moved us to Baltimore City from the suburbs when I was about five years old because she wanted "a change of scenery." She refused to accept public housing due to the horrible living conditions that friends had told her about. We lived above a tiny, corner store in a very small, but neat three-room apartment with one bedroom, one bathroom, and an eat-in kitchen. Mom kept a very clean place and she enjoyed preparing delicious meals for her family. In retrospect, my mother showed her love by never missing parent conferences or performances at the school.

My experiences with my mother have helped me more than I ever realized, because I can better relate to students I have taught. That includes students in high poverty and/or low-performing schools, as well as those students from middle-class homes with blended families.

When I was fifteen years old, my mom married a remarkable man and outstanding teacher, shortly after my father's marriage to my strong stepmother. Over time, I came to love and appreciate my new parents. In fact, they have each taught me some critical lessons about life that have really helped with building personal and professional relationships.

During my teaching experience, I have become less tolerant of people who make assumptions about children and their families based on their living situations or finances. I grew up in a single-parent home in the inner city, attended public school and a local university, and I was able to obtain a successful career in education. I attended a college with several scholarship awards, not due to my grades, because I was not a straight-A student. I received scholarships because I did fairly well in school and I was involved in other extracurricular activities. I never missed a meal or came to school without the necessary materials, because my father worked two jobs seven days a week to provide me with what I needed. My parents and other family members worked together to help me in any way they could. I am so blessed to have people in my life who have helped me to reach and obtain the greatest achievement: the ability to see beyond circumstances and see the talents

and potential of my students. This is what I hope I am able to give to every student who enters my classroom.

———

Story #3

"I do not want to be a teacher like my mother!" Have you ever heard that statement before? Well, that was my statement every time someone would ask what I was going to be when I grew up or what my major was going to be in college. I purposely did not choose education and chose pre-med biology. Who would believe that no matter how much I tried to fight within, my home experiences account for how and why I made decisions then and even now.

Growing up was at times difficult but finally rewarding. My brother and I grew up in a middle-class family. We were able to have more experiences and most things that others didn't. We did not realize the rewarding part until later in life. My parents divorced when I was eight years old. The breakup broke my heart and it still hurts till this day. I was truly a daddy's girl and still am. One thing I can say is that my mother made sure that my father did his part financially and emotionally, but, more importantly, she made sure that we respected him.

My parents were quite different; my mother earned two degrees and my father never finished high school. She also was the dominant figure in our household, the disciplinarian, and made all the decisions regarding my brother and me even when my father was in the household. My friends would say "she ain't a joke."   Nothing, and I mean nothing, got past my mother. Early, I knew not to bring home bad grades and not to be trouble in school; however, I was just hell on wheels at home, especially when it came to boys. My mother's decision to not let me party all the time and hang out with the wrong crowd was truly a reflection on my actions after school in high school. I stayed in trouble at home but was an honor student at school. I was also too scared of my mother not to be a good student and I acted accordingly while in public. At the age of fifteen, I decided that my rebellious attitude was getting me nowhere, so I made a change for the better.

In the early years growing up I would often go to my mother's school where her classroom was always meticulously decorated and bright. I would watch her engage her students with so much excitement about learning. Not only were the students engaged with her strong personality and enthusiasm for learning, parents were also very involved. Oftentimes she would leave her classroom and tell me to watch the kids. I would then go to the front of the class and mimic her. I could walk, talk, and write like her and I must say I did a very good job. To my amazement, I would have the kids just as engaged in the lesson as she would, and I was only in junior high school. Even having that gift at an early age, I tried my best not to go into the education field.

My mother was a great and influential educator in the DC public school system, yet my brother and I went to parochial school. My mother always told us, "Public is for all and private is for few." I always took that to heart. She

was very proud for sacrificing for my brother and me so that we could go to parochial school, yet she worked in the neighborhood public schools near the school my brother and I attended. I never asked and knew not to ask her why I was going to parochial school when she worked in the public schools. I believe to this day that within her heart she saw something back then in the education system and she did not want my brother and me to be a part of it. Even though she felt she could and would personally make a change in her students' lives—in addition to all the challenges and obstacles she faced during her career—public school was not for my brother and me.

While trying to find myself after college and after leaving during my first year of medical school, I found myself cautiously going on interview after interview. One day, while having lunch with my mother at her school, I met the principal of a local junior high school. After a brief and overwhelming conversation with her, my life changed in one swoop. She gave me my first teaching job as a special education teacher. I took the job, thinking it was temporary, because I simply needed to pay my bills.

I went into the classroom blinded, but not that blinded. I did what I knew best; I mimicked my mother and, believe it or not, it worked. I perfected my mother's style and put a twist of my own in there and before I knew it, I was becoming quite successful. I continued to teach in the field of science because biology was my background.

My mentor came to videotape a lesson I was teaching. I knew that I would be critiqued, but did not know to what extent. What I did not realize was that my mother critiqued my video, because she was my supervisor at the school. She made some comments about my teaching style and suggestions on what I needed to do to be successful in this business. I took everything to heart and finally, when she stood up in the class amid my professor, my mentor, and peers, I was holding my breath. She made several comments, but all I heard her say was that she was very proud of me and what I had accomplished in a short time and that she knew I would be successful in education. Whatever else she was saying did not matter except for the fact that she was proud of me. I knew and everyone else knew she was a master teacher and I had learned from the best.

During my third year teaching and having left the junior high school to work in a public school in the suburbs of Maryland, a doctor spoke to my class during career day about the human body. He asked the children many questions and they answered all of them without default. That afternoon, after seeing all five of my classes, he said to me, "Whatever you are doing in your classes for these children to be so confident and knowledgeable, keep doing it." Finally, right then, I knew I had that passion and was in the right profession, educating children.

Early, I fought hard not to be like my mother in so many ways but the battle was lost. I became an educator

anyway and an exceptional one at that. I know that I have touched many children's lives over the last eighteen years.

Some of my students are now young adults with their children. When former students see me they ask if I am still playing music in my classroom. When this happens, I smile, knowing that they remember my unique motivation technique that inspired them to succeed in science, a subject that many students have little interest in.

I wanted to take it a step further and go to graduate school. However, I did not have the gall to ask my mother to pay for it, knowing that she paid for my four years of college. Yes, I was blessed. No grants or scholarships, just a check in hand from my mother. For that, I am truly grateful to her, so I paid for graduate school myself by working extremely hard. It took five years but I finished with a master's degree in administration and supervision. Quickly, I became an Assistant Principal with many other leadership roles to follow. But because of the love for my daughter Baily and my family, I chose to return back to classroom as a teacher and a part-time adjunct professor at Trinity University.

I am currently an educator in the public school system and, as my mother did, I send my daughter to private school. Because of the experiences and challenges that I have faced daily, I do not want my daughter to be a part of the public school system. I believe I was brainwashed about the public school system early in my life. Will Baily have or get a better education? Maybe or maybe not, but I

am very proud to make the same sacrifices my mother did for my brother and me.

———

Story #4

I always felt like an outsider around my family but when I was in school I felt like I truly belonged. My talents of singing, speech/debate, and leadership were first acknowledged by a teacher. On each level of schooling there was a teacher who took me under his/her tutelage and made me feel loved. These individuals made me feel as though I could be successful at anything. When I was in their classes I strived to make the best grades; I listened to their every word. I asked them questions and they answered them no matter how personal they were. I loved the fact that they cared for me, a person of no biological connection to them. My relationships with these educators were some of the best experiences of my life. The connections with my teachers helped me to understand the importance of developing positive relationships with students.

I was extremely fortunate to have so many people in my life who nurtured my being. My mother provided a positive example of what it meant to have a work ethic and be committed to one's education at all cost. My grandmother stressed the importance of my being as peaceable as possible, not allowing others to anger me. My father and stepmother have supported me during my years in college and actively participate in activities associated

with my career as an educator. My college godmother is always there to listen to my concerns, my dreams, and goals. My aunt is always there to be supportive and offer humor when I need it. I have close friends who provide that nonjudgmental ear. There have been so many people (educators, supervisors, and professional and personal mentors) in my life who have nourished me and because of this I believe it is my responsibility to be an advocate for youth. It is important for me to provide the same kind of support to today's African-American youth as I received.

We are living at a time in which African-American youth are failing. They are not moving to the level they should. On the national level their academic achievement is low, levels of suspensions are high, high school graduation rates are low, standardized test scores are low, college graduation rates are low, and incarceration rates are high. African-Americans are often told overtly and/or covertly that they cannot succeed. We have come in contact with adults of all races interacting with our youths in such negative ways that they are truly hazardous. We know them. They are in our schools. They are our neighbors. They are in our churches.

Are we stopping them from putting their toxic beliefs and/or actions upon our African-American youth? No. Can we stop them? Definitely! We must begin by developing adults (of all races and backgrounds) who truly want to assist African-American youth in becoming the best they possibly can be. The adults who commit to our youths must understand the importance of setting high and realistic expectations. They must not be afraid of our youths. They must be willing to go above and beyond at all times. The adults must be willing to give 110 percent to our youths.

For example, I once had a meeting with a mother and daughter. Mrs. Smith and Kim had been having conversations at home over a period of months about how terrible the middle school was where I was an assistant principal. As I listened to Kim and Mrs. Smith express their discontent with the middle school, I began to think about how negative they were. I had never seen the mother volunteer in our building and the student was not the most personable child. I wanted to tell them to get out of my office with all their complaints but I gave them an hour of my time to vent. After they left, I felt deflated, not because I had not changed their minds to stay, but because of how they expressed their dislike of the "bad children." The Smiths did not want students around who did not listen the first time they were told something, who did not comprehend on the first day of instruction, or who did not follow every rule every day. They seemed to want a school of "Stepford" students.

I did not become an educator to berate and degrade children. I became an educator to assist those who need assistance. I became an educator to empower those who are not empowered. I became an educator to teach those

students who are often told they cannot learn. I became an educator as a salute and thank you to all the educators who invested in me so that I could invest in other people's children.

———

Story #5

One of the biggest complaints I hear and one that teachers often make is that parents just don't care these days. Any teacher will tell you what schools in their county or district have parents who are "too" involved. At times teachers feel these overly involved parents can be worse than the nonexistent ones.

I went to school in one of "those counties" where parent involvement was high. My mother, the teacher, knew the power of student advocacy. Being in the system, she was aware of how students are tracked in public schools. My parents wanted the best for me and I knew that I needed to perform at my best in school. As a result, my grades were always high and test scores matched. My good grades and test scores made me eligible for gifted and talented classes. In my school system there were five distinct levels: the special education/co-taught level (CT), general education level, honors level (H), gifted and talented (GT), and advanced placement (AP) level. Courses were designated by level. So in one school there could be multiple offerings of the same course but at different levels. For example, there was English 9 CT, English 9, English 9H, English 9GT, and English 9AP. Usually the AP classes were

the higher-level classes taken in the eleventh or twelfth grade year. Depending on the school and the resources available, GT and AP classes could be combined. The four levels, excluding AP, were considered equal on transcripts, but had very different curricula and expectations.

We were new to the county, as we had moved there from our overseas assignment. Usually the tracking is done in elementary school in the fourth or fifth grade, and I had missed it, as I was entering the sixth grade. My mother went to the school and said she wanted me placed in the GT classes. I vaguely remember there being some resistance and the school needing transcripts and test scores. I did not take standardized tests overseas in the Department of Defense school, so I had to take those tests and be evaluated. I was finally placed into the gifted and talented classes. My schedule was changed and without knowing it then my future was changed. At the time I didn't think anything of it, but looking back, being in this high-level track was both a gift and a curse.

From September of sixth grade to the last day of my twelfth-grade year, I was in classes with the same thirty-five to forty students. It was like we were our own little private school inside of public school. Each class had about twenty-five to thirty students in it and we were almost always the only GT class in any subject at the school. There were hardly any behavior problems and we had limited interaction with students outside of our cohort. Due to the demographic of the school and county, I found myself as one of a handful

of African-Americans in the cohort. The only time we would intermingle with "regular" students was during lunch or in the electives like gym or music. This interaction was, for the most part, limited because of scheduling. It only makes sense that kids with GT schedules would have electives with each other too because of how the schedule was set up.

It was hard being new and one in a sea of many in this new structure. I, of course, befriended those students I spent the majority of the day with, Caucasian students. I coincidentally did not live near many African-American students, so I couldn't hang with them in the neighborhood. This put me in a very interesting situation. The African-American students I encountered were in my homeroom, on my sports teams, and in my electives. I didn't have the benefit of knowing them from elementary school like my other GT African-American classmates. Many of them still kept that tie even though our "intellectual level" segregated us. What my parents didn't know or couldn't have known when they signed me up for these advanced classes is that I was alienated from the other African-American kids. Those other African-American kids, mainly because I was new, viewed me as stuck-up or snobby. I was constantly told that I had "sold out." I would occasionally get a chance to meet African-American kids outside of the cohort through those in the cohort. Every time I met them they would say the same thing, "Oh, girl, I thought you were bourgesie, cuz you don't hang with black folks." I was always so shocked, because I never got a warm reception from any of these other African-

American girls when I tried to hang during lunch or in an elective. In some cases the girls would confront me about being a "phony" and a "sellout." It would hurt my feelings because these girls thought that I consciously decided not to be in classes with them. They didn't even know me and were judging me.

I had no relationship with any African-American girls except the ones in my cohort. Even the girls on my sports teams would be sociable on the field, but would ignore me in the halls. I couldn't understand why I was being penalized for my ability to test well and my work ethic. As a result high school was a miserable time. Everyone wants to be popular and well liked. I think that I could have accepted not being accepted by the African-American community if I had wronged a person or was chubby or in some way unattractive, but being out solely based on something I couldn't control hurt. To compound the issue my extended family, cousins, aunts, and uncles continuously commented on how "white" I'd become. I was deemed "white" because I spoke proper English and played soccer and lacrosse. "Where are your black friends?" was always the question.

By the time high school came, because of how the African-American girls in school treated me, I didn't want any African-American friends. I was fine without them and they didn't have to accept me. I didn't reject them or make it known how I felt; I just stopped trying to hang. I would be sociable, talk to those few who were in my elective classes, and went on with my life. I also knew that something was

missing in my relationships with my non-African-American friends. There was always a barrier. I could never really express my true self and feelings, some things they just could never understand.

In my college search, I didn't look at any Historically Black Colleges and Universities. I didn't want to go through the pain of being rejected again. I decided to stick with what I knew. In college, I sought the companionship of the other African-American students. I was not successful in gaining meaningful relationships with them because of my lack of prior experience. They all seemed skeptical of my "trust" in white students. We disagreed on the concept of one or the other. I could have white friends and African-American friends. Sadly, I couldn't intermingle the two groups. So, I was forced to make a choice between the two groups. A lot of the African-American students transferred within a year. Again I found myself an island in a sea of white students, but I was strangely comfortable. Consequently I didn't make many true friendships with African-American women until after college. I can admit that even now it is hard to approach African-American women and relate. I feel intimidated and still fear that rejection.

I find it very interesting how the choices parents make or do not make influence their children's lives. Was I prepared for my college career having taken the GT classes? I would say academically, yes; however, I feel that socially I was a bit behind. Each person is a product of his or her

experiences. I'm not sure how my experiences affect my teaching style. I hope that I can be an advocate for ensuring that students don't become one-dimensional. Students need not only academic enrichment, but social and cultural enrichment as well.

Tell Your Story

What experiences do you have that made you the teacher you have become?

_____

_____

_____

_____

_____

_____

_____

_____

_____

_____

_____

_____

_____

_____

_____

_____

_____

_____

_____

_____

_____

_____

_____

_____

Connecting with Youth Quiz

Connecting with Youth: How well do you connect?
This test is designed to assess your level of connection with the youth you interact with. Regardless of your score, you must know that it is never too late to make a change.

1. A student becomes disruptive in class. You…
   a. Immediately reach for your discipline referral.
   b. Restate the rule and then speak with him privately
   c. Scream in his face. You have to fight fire with fire.
   d. Ignore it for now. You don't like confrontation.

2. A student habitually comes late to your class. You…
   a. Ignore it. The halls are really crowded.
   b. Make it a point to embarrass him in front of the class.
   c. Give the consequence based on the norms you've established.
   d. Send the student to the office. Lateness is against school rules

3. A student tests well but turns in no homework. You…
    a. Call home and speak with the parent.
    b. Figure that she has a troubled home life. Better not interfere.
    c. Do nothing. You can't do the homework for her.
    d. Offer an alternative time to help her and other students complete homework before going home.

4. A student consistently comes to class unprepared (without pens, notebook). You…
    a. Take points away from his class work grade.
    b. Put him out of class. He's just being disrespectful.
    c. Ignore it. It's not his fault he's poor.
    d. Talk to him to find out what the issue is.

5. A student bullies other students in the class. You…
    a. Request that student be removed from your class.
    b. Bully that student to break him down.
    c. Don't say anything to him. You don't want to stoop to his level.
    d. Isolate him from the other students.

6. The curriculum you've been teaching for years is rewritten. You…
    a. Put the guide in your desk drawer and keep teaching your way.
    b. Take a look at the new curriculum and incorporate the new strategies.
    c. Teach the new curriculum, but make excuses about it to the students.
    d. Follow the guide to the letter. You don't even have to think anymore.

7. A new student transfers into your class from a neighboring school district that is rumored to be rough. You…
    a. Immediately dread the student coming. You know she'll cause problems.
    b. Think about the last students from that district and put up your guard.
    c. Keep an open mind, each child is different.
    d. Complain to your coworkers about how you get all the problem kids.

8. A well-behaved student seems to be falling behind. You…
    a. Speak with the child and follow up with a parent call.
    b. Ignore it. He'll bounce back.

c. It's OK; he's not a behavior problem.

d. Refer to guidance. You have too many other students to deal with.

9. At a parent-teacher conference you…

a. Give balanced and constructive criticism of the student.

b. Give written comments to the counselor and stay in your classroom. Parents are scary and intimidating.

c. Tell the parent like it is, no holds barred.

d. Wait to hear what other teachers say and agree with them.

10. When making a phone call home to a parent you….

a. Call during your lunch break. You know you'll get the answering machine.

b. Call the work number and complain to whoever answers the phone.

c. Call at six in the morning to ensure that they're home.

d. Prepare for the call by jotting down the important points.

Scoring: 1. a-1, b-0, c-3, d-2; **2.** a-1, b-3, c-0, d-2; **3.** a-1, b-2, c-3, d-0; **4.** a-1, b-2, c-3, d-0; **5.** a-2, b-3, c-1, d-0; **6.** a-3, b-0, c-1, d-2; **7.** a-3, b-2, c-0, d-1; **8.** a-0, b-1, c-2, d-3; **9.** a-0, b-2, c-3, d-1; **10.** a-1, b-3, c-2, d-0.

Turn the page for the results.

Let's find out how connected you are with today's youth. Based on the total score you came up with from the previous page, read your results.

Results

Scores 0 to 7

You are **nontoxic**. You are safe for today's youth. You are employing effective strategies to deal with today's youth. You don't know all the answers and are willing to admit when you don't know answers. You are open to new ideas.

Scores 8 to 15

You are **slightly toxic**. You have good intentions; however, you seem to be fearful of the students. Something is holding you back from reaching your full potential as an instructor or mentor.

Scores 16 to 24

You are **toxic**. You are letting the teaching profession work you instead of you working in the teaching profession. You do the bare minimum to stay afloat. You don't make an effort to do that extra thing that might help your students. It's easier to play it safe is your motto. This laissez-faire approach to teaching perpetuates this cycle of failing youth while the respect your colleagues have for you slowly declines.

Scores 25 to 30

You are a **highly toxic**. You are poisonous to youth. You exhibit an attitude that is confrontational with the students. You may see your style as necessary to break these rough children or keep them in line. This tough and gruff exterior alienates the students and quickly makes enemies of parents, coworkers, and administrators.

Power Play

"Often students are baited by teachers/staff to respond in a negative manner. Students often feel picked on...I have seen teachers prewrite referrals for students, hoping they will do something wrong so they can be put out of the class."

–A Permanent Substitute

Power Play

Research has proven that children need to feel the care and support of loved ones as they develop and grow into confident adults. Childhood experiences must include security, guidance, love, and acceptance. When adults fail to provide children with these necessities the children develop poor self-images. Facing anger, pain, and disappointment is essential for changing one's behavior or mind-set. When we don't address the reason for those negative feelings, we allow those negative feelings to guide our actions and our thinking. They have an incredible effect on the relationships that we form with others. They affect how a person relates to loved ones, colleagues, and associates. This statement is particularly true for adults who teach children. When people's interactions are adversely affected, the feelings of anger, pain, and disappointment may be displayed as a desire to control others and the situations around them.

During this section of the book, we have included scenarios from our teaching careers that show how some of the feelings from individuals' pasts have impacted the choices or decisions made within the school environment. More specifically, the scenarios show how there is often a direct correlation between individuals' actions and their feelings of anger, pain, or disappointment. Each scenario includes mistakes made, strategies that worked, and lessons learned in each situation. If you look carefully at each scenario you will see a clear correlation between the backgrounds of the individuals involved and their reactions. The stories

are included to help other teachers, mentors, and parents analyze and reflect on their interactions with children. Our intention is to help them develop more positive responses to inappropriate behaviors without getting into power struggles. We found that looking at our own shortcomings has been one of the greatest tools for strengthening our relationships with students and improving our abilities as teachers.

Scenario #1

Jamal informed Ms. Jones that Trina knocked his binder on the floor. Ms. Jones told the two students that someone needed to hurry up and pick up the binder from the floor or she would throw it into the trash can. Jamal pleaded with Trina to pick up the binder. Ms. Jones saw that neither student wanted to pick up the binder so she picked it up and put it in the trash can. Jamal then asked Ms. Jones if he could go to the office to see the assistant principal.

Think about it.

List some of the positive actions/behaviors. What went wrong in the scenario? What things could have been done differently?

_____

_____

_____

_____

_____

_____

_____

_____

_____

_____

_____

_____

_____

_____

_____

_____

_____

_____

_____

_____

_____

_____

_____

_____

The scenario explained:

Looking at this scenario it would appear that no positive action took place; however, the student followed the chain of command in his attempt to get his problem solved. He first asked his peer to pick up the notebook, then the teacher, and finally he requested the assistance of the assistant principal. The greatest mistake in this scenario was that the teacher did not listen to the student. She demonstrated no patience and an overall lack of sensitivity to the situation. She obviously does not respect the student. Many will argue that the teacher acted this way as to not further disrupt the lesson; however, instead of throwing the notebook away she could have picked up, placed in a safe place, and discussed the situation at a later date. The lack of respect demonstrated by the teacher destroyed any relationship between herself and the student. Breaking the trust a student has in the teacher's ability to handle minor situations can be detrimental to interactions with this student and others in the class. The student will respond by exhibiting poor academic performance and possible future behavioral problems.

"From my experiences with teachers I have learned that you have to have compassion for your students and you have to know where the students are coming from. Whenever I interact with students they get my full attention. I give them eye contact; I listen to what they have to say. I don't always agree, but I always listen."

–A Veteran Teacher

Scenario #2

Omar was a fourteen-year-old student in an alternative school in Chicago. Ms. Boote was Omar's Spanish teacher at this school. Ms. Boote had met Omar during the summer when she taught classes to youths who were staying in a foster home. So they started off having a positive interaction with each other because of their prior knowledge of each other. Ms. Boote noticed that Omar seemed to be very confrontational with other teachers and staff members in the school. Ms. Boote, in her second-year teaching wisdom, would often state that Omar should never speak to her in that manner and if he did she would teach him a thing or two.

One day Omar was not in the best of moods. Ms. Boote asked him to answer a question and he refused to answer. Ms. Boote then asked Omar if he had a problem and he said; "Yes–you." Ms. Boote then stated, "I do not know who you think you are talking to. Get out of my class." Omar got up, knocked over the desk, and said, "Fuck you, bitch," as he was leaving the classroom. Ms. Boote went after him and got in his face and repeated, "I do not know who you think you are talking to." Omar responded, "You, bitch," as he raised his hand toward Ms. Boote. Ms. Boote grabbed Omar's hand and used her free hand to push him away from her.

Think about it.

List some of the positive actions/behaviors. What went wrong in the scenario? What things could have been done differently?

_____
_____
_____
_____
_____
_____
_____
_____
_____
_____
_____
_____
_____
_____
_____
_____
_____
_____
_____
_____
_____

The scenario explained:

This scenario started out very positively with the relationship that developed between Ms. Boote and Omar during the summer program. The scenario went awry when Ms. Boote failed to take the opportunity to assist Omar in the transition from the summer program to the school setting. She also failed to communicate to Omar that it was inappropriate to speak to any adult in the manner in which he did. By ignoring the negative interactions Omar was having with her coworkers, she sent the message that this behavior was acceptable. The final issue with this scenario is the escalation that took place between the teacher and student. When a student escalates, the teacher should do the exact opposite and become calm. You can always revisit the situation at a later time. When the teacher noticed there was a problem, she should not have confronted the student. We need to remember to always pick a time and place for all interactions. The middle of class was not the appropriate time to deal with this issue.

Scenario #3

Another Friday was here and this Friday was special. We were showing movies, and not just any movie, but the latest movie complete with snacks and candy!!!! Gary and a few other students wanted to be a part of it; however, they had either missed too many homework assignments or decided to talk back at the wrong time. Because of this,

they had to go to a special room where there was no movie and no snacks. Of course none of them were happy to be excluded from the festivities. But Gary kept his signature smirk and quick tongue as he showed his disgust about being excluded while trying to appear not to care at the same time. But as I walked him to the room where he would be while we watched the movie, my foot slipped and I almost fell. OK, laugher was to be expected but Gary's outburst went over the top. I looked at him with disgust and he replied, "What, I can't laugh at you?" My quick-tongued response..."HELL NO, you can't laugh at me!"

Think about it.
How could this situation have been handled differently?
List some of the positive actions/behaviors.

_____

_____

_____

_____

_____

_____

_____

_____

_____

_____

The scenario explained:

In this scenario the teacher allowed her frustration to not only show, but to escalate into something that could have ended her career in an instant. She took herself entirely too seriously. A common mistake is that a first-year teacher has to be serious in order to be respected. In fact, the student and teacher could have both laughed, and he still would have gone in the room and missed the movie.

———

Scenario #4

Day after day the role is called and every student responds to the sound of his or her name with the word "here," all except one. "Darnell, is Darnell here?" Wow that's two weeks now he has not been here after calls to his mother and home visits; despite the intervention of social services, we still have not seen him in class. Not to mention this will be his second year in the sixth grade. For the past two years Darnell's teachers have begun the referral process on him. They recognize a severe deficit in his reading and written responses. However, the desired special education referral was never reached. So year after year he would return with a larger gap between where his reading level should be and where he was, a larger body, and a more streetwise outlook. This year he decided school was simply a waste of time.

When Darnell made his great return to school I let him know that I had his back. I explained that he and I would work together to get him to learn everything necessary to

move forward and get to where he belonged, which was not in the sixth grade again! He seemed pleased to hear it. But rather than sitting and allowing me to proceed with the day's lesson he began telling everyone about his time spent in the juvenile detention center and about his parole officer. When I would redirect him and let him know that I was teaching class so he needed to save his conversation for another time he would respectfully say…"OK, Mrs. G," but would go right back to talking to anyone who would listen. This type of behavior continued daily for months. At times he would walk around and take items off of students' desks. Day after day he interrupted lessons and ignored requests to allow me, the teacher, to teach class. Go figure! He never completed an assignment and made countless empty promises to complete them. He would be assigned detentions, which he never attended, and rarely received disciplinary action because no one wanted to send him back home; the goal is to keep him in school, is it not? At any rate students soon became terrorized by his constant talking, throwing of pencils, erasers, and other objects. They also continually found items missing, yelling his name out in response. "Darnell took my pencil! Darnell has my pen. Darnell stole my book," on and on; it seemed to never end. Meanwhile he never completed an assignment except during one-on-one situations with me and then it would involve small assignments. Darnell would throw tantrums if he was not allowed time to surf the Web or play games at will. So how did I handle this?

Public humiliation is what I decided to use. I needed to bully the bully. When he would yell out about his latest fight posted on YouTube I would let him know. "OK, well, unless you're ready for a fight between me and you to be posted, you need to be quiet and let me work." He and the class would laugh and I would be allowed to teach. But the problem would continue. More importantly his reading level did not improve and his behavior was so out of control I was unable to even give him any assessments to determine progress on any level.

Think about it.

What was the power play in this situation? What could have been done differently? Do you agree with how the situation was handled? Why or why not?

_____

_____

_____

_____

_____

_____

_____

_____

_____

_____

The scenario explained:

The teacher never involved Darnell's parents. She made countless assumptions about his mother based on information from previous teachers and faculty members who personally knew his family. The teacher decided it was best to learn to "handle" him herself. This worked in getting to know him and building a relationship with him. She failed to realize that no matter how insignificant the parenting may appear, all parents should receive constant updates of their children's progress.

She assumed that he would respect her for getting in his personal space, speaking to him in his "street" language, and letting him know that she would take care of him. If he respected the teacher it would allow her to take him to the next level. This may have worked if she didn't have twenty-five other students to work with.

Scenario # 5

Lindsey wanted to keep a small container of juice in her desk. The rule in Ms. Jenkins' class was to store all snacks and lunches on the lunch counter to alleviate any problems with leaks inside of the students' desks. The rule was also put into place to cut back on unwanted critters, such as roaches and mice, which they battled on a daily basis. Lindsey lied and said that she didn't have any food or drinks in her desk, but the teacher saw her juice container. The seven-year-old student refused to place her container of juice on the appropriate counter or admit that she had it inside her desk.

So, Ms. Jenkins quickly removed the container of juice and slammed it on the lunch counter. "I want my juice!" Lindsey shouted. The teacher reminded Lindsey that every student must put his or her lunch or snack on the counter. "Leave me alone!" the girl screamed. The teacher told her to calm down and be quiet because she was interrupting the lesson. "You can sit here quietly and do the lesson with us or you can go to the office and complete it there," said Ms. Jenkins. The student began to scream, this time cursing.

Ms. Jenkins sent a messenger to the office to get the new vice principal, Mrs. Armstrong. Lindsey stood up and turned over her desk and all of its contents. Despite Ms. Jenkins' shock, she told the rest of the students to line up quickly to keep them safe. By the time Mrs. Armstrong arrived to the open-space classroom Lindsey had flipped over at least two more desks. Ms. Jenkins explained the situation, quickly continuing to move the rest of her students into the common area used for serving lunches. Mrs. Armstrong never entered the teacher's area; she stood on the outside of one of the bookshelves that created a wall in this open-space classroom and replied frantically, "You're more equipped to handle her than I am!" Mrs. Jenkins was more astounded by the child's rage than the reaction of this particular administrator. She was sorry she wasted her time and proceeded to leave the area with her other students.

Mrs. Armstrong was left to manage the situation alone, looking dumbfounded from the common area. Ms. Jenkins decided not to leave the useless woman stranded, so she stopped by the office to get another administrator to assist her.

Think about it

What would you have done in this situation? How would you have reacted differently? Have you ever worked with an ineffective leader?

_____

_____

_____

_____

_____

_____

_____

_____

_____

_____

_____

_____

_____

_____

_____

_____

_____

The scenario explained

Don't waste time with those who hold a position but have no real authority. Some administrators merely have a title but not the heart or abilities to handle a crisis situation. They don't have the resources to offer solutions. Some administrators expect teachers to do the work and they take the credit, grin, and nod their approval. There are key players in every building. It is important that you work hand and hand with them when you have a difficult student. Befriend one of the key players; form a bond with a veteran teacher or a teacher with excellent classroom management so that you have a support system.

Scenario # 6

After a year or two of teaching, I learned that every child is very different and after having children myself I solidified that as fact. Realizing this, I understand that I must have a discipline plan for my class but the action steps taken for each student cannot be identical. What works for Janet will not work for Jonte, not on a daily basis at least. With Jonte I found that because he thrived on public confrontation, he occasionally needed to be broken down and stripped in front of his peers. A slice of humble pie from time to time, if you will, seemed to benefit him. After a few phone calls and visits from his mother I realized that she needed to stay abreast of behavior and progress but that I had to find away to get the behaviors I desired

and needed to properly function in my classroom on a day-to-day basis.

I rarely come across a student who simply can't be told anything. They have all of the answers and their point of view is the only correct one. Jonte was just that student; talk about a classic love/hate relationship. I almost felt like I was in a somewhat abusive relationship. One moment he was obedient and charming, helpful, and caring. The next minute he was talking back and being disrespectful, confrontational, and rude. Clearly he was accustomed to speaking in a disrespectful tone to adults. This was my perception until I met his mother. She came across as very stern and he appeared to have a great deal of respect for her, despite his "I don't care, call my mother" tantrums.

However, the behaviors did not change. They simply got worse. But I realized that I had to break him down to get into his head to find out what was causing the outbursts. None of my other strategies were working. Although embarrassing him in front of his peers quieted him from time to time that was merely temporary, a Band-Aid on an oozing infected sore. Luckily, our sixth-grade team was assigned a social worker from the city on an anti-teen pregnancy initiative. So she was able to see each of my students in a one-on-one session. Although it was only once a week, and some students were seen only once for the year, it still benefited Jonte. In that setting he opened up about his yearning for a relationship for his father and how the pain from that contributed to his attitude. Though not an excuse to justify his behavior, being able to talk with him about it and discuss a plan for how he and I could work past it in our classroom had the greatest impact.

Think about it.

List some of the positive actions/behaviors. Is the manner in which this teacher interacted with this student acceptable to you? Why or why not?

_____

_____

_____

_____

_____

_____

_____

_____

_____

_____

_____

_____

_____

_____

_____

_____

_____

_____

The scenario explained:

The main failure of this scenario was in assuming that public humiliation works in the long run. I didn't take the time to get to know my student because of the volatile relationship we had. Public humiliation is unnecessary and does not have a long-term impact. If a student must be broken down, do it privately and be sure to build the relationship from it.

———

Scenario # 7

Ms. Bowman's first class was a true test of her patience and skills. However, her neighboring teammate did not help to ease her pain in any way. In fact, she helped to make it miserable. Her class of twenty-two students consisted of twelve girls and ten boys, four of whom she was sure were possessed by Satan himself. Two of them received special education services. The students did whatever they could to taunt the teacher and students. They would throw spitballs, put tacks in students' chairs, and make noises during instruction.

One day Ms. Bowman was prepared to teach the class about vertebrates and invertebrates, when she learned just how cruel her neighbor could be. During her introductory activity, two of the boys began bothering one girl by tapping her and looking away. Ms. Bowman reminded the students to keep their hands to themselves or she would have to take their recess. The boys decided to toss paper at the girl instead, so the teacher moved their seats. She was very careful with her words, for she knew how confrontational they would be if she moved one of them and not the other. "Demetrius and Tobias move to the front of the class quickly," she shouted. Then she redirected each one to a specific seat. Despite the new seating arrangement, the students continued to be disruptive. One began to make animal noises during the lesson and then some of the other students repeated it. It was very frustrating for Ms. Bowman, but she tried to handle the disruptive students and continue the lesson. She put up a silent signal and wrote the names of the disruptive students on the front board under the words "No Recess." Then Demetrius and Tobias began expressing what they felt about recess while many of the other students started talking to their neighbors. Ms. Bowman knew that at this point she would have to redirect the students to the science lesson using another method. Before she could quiet the class, she could hear the annoying voice of her neighbor, Ms. Johns, shouting over, "I wish the students in that class would be quiet, so that my class can learn!" Ignoring the voice, Ms. Bowman reminded the students of the subgroups in the vertebrate group using some actual photographs. Just as she was gaining their attention back she heard the teacher leading her class in the following chant: "I wish that they would be quiet, some of us are trying to learn." Ms. Bowman stopped and reminded the students that they were in an open-space classroom and they must work quietly so they didn't disturb their neighbors. She hoped that this would satisfy

the veteran teacher and shut her up. Ms. Bowman noticed that it was lunchtime and she was relieved to escape it all for at least thirty minutes. She held back the tears until her students were out of sight.

Ms. Bowman was hurt by her colleague's harsh approach, but certainly was not shocked, as this was not the first time that this had happened. Ms. Bowman decided that she would never be respected by her students and have control over her class as long as this horrible woman was near her.

Think about it.

How would you have handled the students in this situation? How would you have addressed the other teacher? Have you ever been disrespected by an adult in front of your class?

_____

_____

_____

_____

_____

_____

_____

_____

_____

The scenario explained:

Ms. Bowman realized that she allowed the other teacher to belittle her in front of her class because she did not address the matter when it first occurred. Instead of telling her colleague about how she made her feel, Ms. Bowman walked around keeping everything to herself. It is important to address a problem rather than let it continue or escalate. By not addressing the other teacher's behavior, she was accepting it. She learned that she must consult someone else when she felt that a situation with a colleague was affecting her ability to complete her tasks.

Power Play Conclusion

Occasionally teachers have the terrible misconception that classroom management means yelling at students and ruling with an iron fist. As seen in the scenarios presented and possibly through your own experiences, classroom management involves a lot more than just correcting students or raising your voice. The scenarios were designed to show you that the relationship between student and teacher is just as important as the classroom rules that are established. School should be a place where students feel welcomed, included, and secure. When teachers use their power inappropriately, that sense of security is threatened.

Psychologists Jan N. Hughes and Timothy A. Cavell of Texas A&M University conducted a study on the correlation between student behavior and student-teacher relationship. The study found that the chance of aggressive

behavior recurring was reduced when a student at risk for behavioral problems and the teacher maintained a warm and close relationship. Hughes indicates that the study gives strong evidence that a positive teacher-student relationship can have a lasting effect. The study found that the "better the teacher-student relationship was for a given year, the greater the chances of that student not being viewed as aggressive by his or her peers the next year" (Milburn, 2004).

Originally it was thought that a teacher should be tougher or harder on those misbehaving students. The Hughes-Cavell study indicates the opposite. The study found that teacher-student interactions with high level of conflict and controlling interactions coupled with low levels of warmth and acceptance increased the student's risk for aggressive behavior. Hughes explains, "Generally, aggressive children receive more criticism because they invite more opportunities for conflict. When a student is often in conflict with the teacher, he or she feels less motivated to please the teacher and less motivated to conform to classroom rules. These students feel less of a sense of belonging with the school." Hughes and Cavell also note that the cycle of a negative teacher-student relationship and the increase of aggression seem endless as one aggravates the other. A similar study was conducted by Dr. Ramon Lewis of La Trobe University. In his study he found that the students were quick to pick up the hint of dislike and rejection, which led to the deterioration of their behavior. Dr. Lewis states,

"It's important for teachers locked in this spiral (conflicted teacher-student relationship) to recognize that the only behavior they can control is their own. If they can do that then the child is more likely to cooperate."

This chapter on power plays is intended to inspire you to take control of your own actions when dealing with the youth in your lives. In your interactions with your students, youth groups, or mentees be sure to communicate acceptance and warmth. Building a positive relationship is truly the only power you need to be effective.

Judging Books by Covers

"I see a lot of pre judging. I see teachers often pre judge their students. And one place that I find to be very negative is the teacher's lounge…'Oh those poor kids' or 'well you know I'm hoping that on Friday they will bring their money in, cause Thursday is the first and their parents get their checks." Or I hear, "you know John doesn't live with his father because he's incarcerated, or his mother got arrested last night… don't they look dirty? Yeah, they don't look so clean…I just feel like a lot of times the children are prejudged before they even get a chance to perform or show who they really are."

–A Paraprofessional

Judging Books by Covers

How we interact with youth is strongly determined by the prejudgments we hold whether we are aware of them or not. Our prejudices come from a variety of sources. They stem from our personal experiences, upbringings, interactions, and unfortunately they often stem from gossip or things we've "heard." In many cases we are unaware of our prejudices and how they negatively impact children. It is critical that we can each be critically reflective when facing our possible prejudices.

In the following set of scenarios we will demonstrate situations where subconscious and often unconscious pre-judgments based on race, gender, socio economic status and other factors impact an adult's ability to interact appropriately with the youth they seek to serve.

———

Scenario #1

Troy was a sixth-grader attending a small public school in which school uniforms were required. The students were required to wear a solid polo shirt that was black, maroon, or gray. Every other day Troy entered the school wearing a nonuniform shirt. On these days Troy was sent to the office to speak to the administrator and given a school uniform shirt to wear for the day. Troy was given three polo shirts and a sweatshirt to keep.

Over a couple of weeks, Troy continued to be out of uniform despite being given shirts of his own. One day the administrator, having reached her limits, asked Troy why he was he unable to come to school dressed, even though he had been given uniform shirts to keep. Troy had no answer. This angered the administrator. She brought Troy to her office and then to his home. When his mother answered, the administrator explained that Troy had been consistently not in uniform. Troy's mother replied, "I tell him to wash his uniform shirt every night." Troy's home had no washer or dryer, forcing him to wash his clothes by hand every night.

Think about it.

What went wrong in the scenario? What things could have been done differently? What assumptions were made about Troy? How did these assumptions affect the interaction between Troy and the administrator? What can be done to remedy the solution now that the true problem has been revealed?

_____

_____

_____

_____

_____

_____

_____

The scenario explained:

After this conversation the administrator attended a community meeting and discussed the uniform policy. The administrator was informed that the self-service laundry in the community is open Monday–Friday from 8:00 a.m.–5:00 p.m. These hours of operation are based on the time during which the leasing office was open. The mother's work hours are 8:00 a.m.–6:00 p.m. Monday–Friday. In an effort to better serve the students, the administrator and staff created a uniform loaner system so that students would not have to worry about being out of uniform because of circumstances outside of their control.

———

Scenario #2

An eighth-grade teacher, whom I will call Barbara, thought of how she enjoyed working with her 180 students. She reflected on how they seemed interested and engaged in the various learning activities each class period. She was quite impressed with how they stayed on task most of the time. Of course, there were some children who were more challenging than others, one in particular, a boy named Marquise. Barbara noticed that Marquise had a short attention span, had difficulty completing a task, and was quite disruptive. In fact, Barbara was quite frustrated and angry with Marquise. She, however, continued in her efforts, trying a variety of teaching and behavior management strategies, which led to little or no significant change. One

day, after a few months of little or no progress, Barbara came to the exasperation point and, thinking aloud, she muttered, "You know, Barbara, you can't save them all." Because of her statement, Marquise became quite angry and walked out. Because he walked out she immediately began the process to get him tested for special education.

Later it was discovered that Marquise did well in all his other classes. He just did not get along with some of the children in the class; therefore he was being disruptive in her class. When his schedule was changed to another class Barbara finally saw that he was not disruptive and could stay on task and complete all the assignments given.

Think about it.

Do you believe "you can't save them all"? Why or why not?

How does the insightful or dedicated educator constructively teach in a developmentally appropriate way to meet the varying needs of a diverse student population?

_____

_____

_____

_____

_____

_____

_____

_____

_____

_____

_____

_____

_____

_____

_____

_____

_____

_____

_____

The scenario explained:

In this scenario, the teacher did not take the appropriate actions needed to diagnose the problem. The teacher made a judgment about Marquise without doing the necessary research. The teacher should have asked her team members or Marquise's other teachers about his behavior before hastily filling out the special education referral. She would have then been able to diagnose the problem by dealing with the group dynamic instead of alienating one student. When the teacher made the comment about not "saving them all," it angered the student, because he knew that she had falsely categorized him. When students see that teachers unfairly make assumptions about them or others, their trust is diminished. No positive relationship can exist when there is a lack of trust

---

Scenario # 3

Mr. Newman had been teaching for a total of ten years and he loved it! He was respected for his ability to manage his class and teach them writing. This year's third-grade class had some awesome math students, but very few excellent writers. In fact, this class of twenty students had only two really outstanding writers. Both of the writers who stood out were female. So, Mr. Newman thought about how he would have to really work to improve their skills. He was excited about the challenge. Mr. Newman made such a big deal about the students' finished products that the students gained a passion for writing and sharing their work.

One day the students were working on personal narratives about a time when they were afraid, and Mr. Newman made a wonderful discovery. He was circulating around the room assisting students with revising their rough drafts. Though Mr. Newman had a way of making all of his students feel like they were remarkable writers, he didn't believe it to be true about two students in particular, Samuel and Gabrielle. On this day, Mr. Newman was hesitating about getting to table two because he dreaded trying to make sense of Samuel's chicken scratch. Mr. Newman thought that his speech problems tremendously affected his writing. The student was a struggling reader so that didn't help him. He assumed that his narrative would be just a bunch of unreadable mumbo jumbo. Mr. Newman smiled and prepared himself as he lifted the scrawny, bright-eyed boy's paper. Samuel, as he almost always did, asked the teacher if he could he read his story. The teacher had a little difficulty reading the boy's handwriting, but he asked the boy to read the parts that he didn't understand.

Mr. Newman was not only surprised, but he was impressed by the level of vocabulary words the young boy included in his delightful narrative. He made a few changes with the student to help him with his final draft. Then Mr. Newman complimented him for taking risks with his spelling. Finally, he asked Samuel to read his story to the class.

Think about it.

What effective teaching strategies did you notice? How would you describe the teacher's behavior? What assumptions have you made about students in your class? Has your bias affected your students' performance?

_____

_____

_____

_____

_____

_____

_____

_____

_____

_____

_____

_____

_____

_____

_____

_____

_____

_____

_____

_____

_____

The scenario explained:

Mr. Newman learned that you must always give students an opportunity to demonstrate their abilities. He understood that although students may have limitations in a particular subject area it doesn't mean that they can't persevere to do great things. Bias toward any student can limit progress and diminish a student's self-esteem. Mr. Newman had a disposition that allowed his students to know that they were unique and talented, which helped to hide or overshadow his bias. We must remember that we, as teachers, must help to enhance our students' skills and encourage all of our students with every lesson plan. These two elements must be evident from the introductory activity to the closure of a lesson.

———

Scenario #4

As I previewed my class list for the upcoming school year one name stood out among the rest. I looked at it over and over again. "OH, GREAT!" I said to myself. Having worked with teachers in the pre-referral process for two years I had become extremely familiar with his name. He was documented as being behind grade level by at least three years in reading and at least two years in math. His behavior was described as torturous by one teacher. Parent involvement was rarely documented. I immediately said, "OK, he's all yours and you are going to have to put together

a plan to work with him. Obviously this won't be a case where the parent and I will work together. I'm on my own."

I never involved his parents. I made countless assumptions about his mother based on information from previous teachers and faculty members who knew his family personally. I decided that I was best off learning to "handle" him myself, which worked in getting to know him and building a somewhat respectful relationship with him. But I failed to realize that no matter how insignificant the parenting appears to be, all parents should receive constant updates of their children's progress. Truancy became an issue. I am ashamed to say that I was relieved by his high number of absences. However, weeks and even months would pass with no sign of him. I assumed that he had just gone to another school and that was that. He returned and he did no class work, no homework, and constantly bullied students. In talking to him and handling him with mutual respect he came to be very fond of me as a teacher. But he still drove me crazy with disruptions, outbursts, and his poor work ethic. I endured all of these things but never contacted his parent. One day his mother contacted the school. She told me of a physical condition she had, which prevented her from visiting the school, and how it has kept her back from keeping track of her son's behavior and academic performance. She apologized profusely. I felt ashamed. I was told and had assumed she didn't care.

Think about it.

What type of damage control must this teacher conduct? Could the parent have said or done something sooner to assist the teacher? What would you have done differently in this scenario?

_____

_____

_____

_____

_____

_____

_____

_____

_____

_____

_____

_____

_____

_____

_____

_____

_____

_____

_____

_____

The scenario explained:

After that phone conference and conversations with the student the teacher learned a valuable lesson. Never judge the situation by its cover or go on someone else's word. Begin every school year with new relationships and get to know every student and parent as if you have never "heard the gossip."

Scenario #5

Jermaine came to school every day fully in uniform and cute as a button. He easily engaged in conversation and seemed to love school. I could see that I was going to enjoy having him in my sixth-grade social studies class. Jermaine was always smiling and pleasant but wow, does he ever sit down? Oh my goodness, I've never seen anyone more distractible than him! Jermaine was constantly out of his seat, under his seat or hanging off the side of his seat. I said to myself, OK, classic attention deficit hyperactivity. Boy, I hope he's learning here. I grew weary and called his mother. We discussed his condition and I told her I was familiar with it and would give him space to be himself. He would be allowed to move freely as long as he didn't talk to or touch other students to distract them. We were all fine with this plan. However, Jermaine was not completing many assignments and I was certain he was not learning the material. So one day after he had been under his desk longer than in it I got aggravated and in a very firm voice said, "Jermaine, you did no work today! What was the lesson about? HUH?" And to my surprise…he gave me a play-by-play retell of every topic covered in class and had restated my objective beautifully. My scowl turned in to a bright smile, I hugged Jermaine and told him how I loved him. I laughed to myself and said, "Looks can be deceiving!" Jermaine had retained more from under his seat than all of the other students had gotten glued to their seats with wandering minds.

Think about it.

How can this teacher empower Jermaine to be an active participant in class lessons? Have you ever assumed a student "just was not getting it" and were then proved wrong? How did you correct yourself?

_____

_____

_____

_____

_____

_____

_____

_____

_____

_____

The scenario explained:

The teacher learned that Jermaine, like many students who suffer from attention deficit hyperactivity disorder, have a unique way of learning. They require an enormous amount of patience and planning. It is crucial to their development to have a teacher who will work cooperatively with their parents to implement a plan that will allow the student to meet with some level of success within the classroom. Research has shown that many of these students have difficulty completing written assignments. They often dislike writing; therefore, a variety of ways should be employed to allow the student to demonstrate his understanding of the lesson. With the assistance of the special educator, teachers can include a number of strategies within his individual education plan. It may also have been helpful for Jermaine to have another place, outside of the classroom, where he could go to work on assignments or do other tasks to release some of his energy.

Judging Books by Covers Conclusion

We are all guilty of making judgments about people we have never met. These judgments can be based on the skin color, manner of dress, or the behavior a particular person exhibits. As seen in the scenarios, acting on these judgments can be dangerous and even detrimental to the youths in our lives. Camille Cooper wrote an article based on the research she conducted with the mothers of African-American males. Her study's findings were startling. Researchers and child psychologists Bartolomew, Solórzano, and Valencia found that a teacher's effectiveness is directly connected to his/her deep-seated beliefs about students' intelligence, character, and potential (Cooper, 2003).

Cooper asserts that due to the judgments made by teachers about their students, the students are susceptible to being harmed by these teachers based on their race, class, gender, and family backgrounds. In her study, Cooper interviewed the mothers of young boys of color. The study showed that these lower-income women of color valued education and were very concerned with their sons' educational careers. This discovery challenges the prior research about African-American and lower-income families. The mothers, through their interviews, cited the emotional and sometimes physical effects.

Cooper asserts that teachers need to be cognizant of judgments and work to overcome them and, more importantly, not to act on their judgments. Students' self-esteem is affected by the actions teachers make based on their judgments. This chapter is designed to help you become aware of the judgments you may be making in your interactions with youths, coworkers, and the community.

Bringing Bias

"In the atmosphere of the building that I work in I often ask myself if the educators in my building even want to be here? Then I feel that for a lot of them this is just a job. Many of them are very negative. It's like, they make their money in the inner city schools and carry it back with them to the suburbs and that's the end of it. It's like they don't take the opportunity to get to know the children… Children emotionally and psychologically sense this. From their adult relationships they feel it."

–A Paraprofessional

Bringing Bias

Bias is defined as a preference toward a particular perspective, ideology, or result. Many studies have been conducted on biases. There are several common forms of biases: class bias, cultural bias, racial bias, religious bias, and gender bias. Numerous researchers have focused on gender bias within the classroom due to the alarming discrepancies in the academic performance between girls and boys. Researchers Myra and David Sadker (1997) identified the following four types of teacher responses in their classroom study: teacher praises, teacher remediates, teacher criticizes, and teacher accepts. Their observations proved that male students received more teacher responses that were classified as praises or remediations. In a more recent study published in the *Journal of Instructional Psychology*, Kelly Jones, Cay Evans, Ronald Byrd, and Kathleen Campbell (2000) found that the use of videotaped lessons allowed teachers to see their own gender biases during their instruction of students. Their recordings also confirmed that teachers often respond more positively to male students than they do to female students.

During this section of the book, we have scenarios that will reveal some of our own experiences with biases. We have decided to reveal to you some of the biases that we have recognized in our own classroom experiences. We want to share with you some valuable lessons that we have learned from examining our instructional practices.

Hopefully, you will be inspired to more carefully examine your responses to students in your classroom. It is natural to display some bias, but as educators, demonstrating equity among our students is essential to their academic success. Research has proven that students are not only affected academically when gender bias is present, they are also affected socially and mentally. In other words, gender bias can cause female students to develop a very negative self-image with very limited projections for the future.

Scenario #1

Often times students, especially African-American males, can be quite defiant and sometime violent. I can remember as a second-year teacher, an African-American male in the seventh grade simply would not cooperate so I asked him to leave my classroom. He said no. I asked him three times and each time he said no. I was quite mad by this time, so I went over to him, grabbed him, and pulled him down the hall. He was kicking and screaming and the more he kicked and screamed the more I dug my fingernails into him.

Think about it.

How could this situation have been handled differently?

List some of the positive actions/behaviors.

_____

_____

_____

_____

_____

_____

_____

_____

_____

_____

_____

_____

_____

_____

_____

_____

_____

_____

_____

_____

The scenario explained:

The first issue to address in this scenario is the teacher's comment about African-American males being defiant and violent. This prejudgment is the basis for the dramatic and uncalled for response. It is never appropriate to use physical force with a defiant student. Luckily, this teacher learned very quickly that there are others in the building to take care of discipline problems and people to help with classroom management.

Scenario # 2

As a teacher for many years, I surely can recall gender bias going on in my classroom. It simply started immediately. I might say it is a girl thing. Most girls in the classroom were very nasty and very hesitant about getting to know their teacher. While the boys, on the other hand, were very friendly. Right then and there, I paid more attention to the boys simply because of their demeanor and the respect that they showed me immediately.

Think about it.

Do you believe gender biases are issues in your school environment?

_____

_____

_____

_____

_____

_____

_____

_____

_____

_____

_____

_____

_____

_____

_____

_____

_____

_____

_____

_____

_____

The scenario explained:

The teacher learned that showing bias toward any students only causes more of a division between the other students and the teacher. For example, during the study session with only the boys she further distanced herself from the girls. Gender bias caused more problems within the room because it stopped her from developing a closer relationship with them. The girls were resentful of the relationship with the boys, and rightfully so, because the teacher was not extending the same courtesies to them. All children, regardless of their gender, need to feel the same level of commitment from their teacher. They also want to feel accepted by their peers; as part of this stage of development.

Students must know that they can trust you before they begin to let you in on the things that matter most to them. Perhaps the teacher could have used a different approach with the girls by inviting them to focus on something that really appealed to them. She could have learned more about their interests, had she spent more time trying to get to know them or by including them in the study sessions. The teacher took on their negative attitude instead of invoking a more positive attitude to form a positive classroom environment.

The teacher in this scenario demonstrated gender bias by deliberately showing favoritism toward the male students in her science class. This situation is very common in science and math classes, despite our willingness to acknowledge it. Several researchers have noted that there are a number of strategies that teachers and other school staff can use to decrease the number of inequities involving gender. A number of strategies have been collected from a variety of resources and can be found at the end of this book.

———

Scenario #3

I had seen Sam around the school for the two years I had been working in this new school district. Sam was a student; he seemed to be a loner but had developed a reputation as an excellent safety patrol. The head of security often joked about how no one could rerun the bus numbers like Sam; he was invaluable. So when I discovered that he was in my class I was happy to have him.

Over time Sam proved to love math but as a special needs student with an IEP, I knew that reading would be an issue. In addition to his avoidance of all reading, which I discovered he could do and do well but just avoided, I also grew weary of his repetitive talking. If he were missing a pencil the whole world would come to an end. If he thought someone teased him on Monday, by Friday I had heard about it a thousand times.

After a few months of this, his teacher from the previous year approached me in the hallway and I asked her about Sam. "Sam loved you; he constantly asks to visit you. Please, tell me how you dealt with him!" I was pleading because, although he was a math wiz, he was also a constant disruption. He was always pointing his finger and claiming that someone had hit him or was teasing him. Yet from what I saw he was constantly teasing and joking with other students. She laughed and asked, "Have you met his mother yet?" My eyes got big and I said, "Oh, no…what do I need to expect?" She proceeded to tell me about a conference where she cursed, screamed, and carried on. I left that conversation believing, OK, that's a parent I will avoid.

A few short weeks later, Sam's taunting of other students escalated into his receiving a suspension. His mother came to the school and we met for the first time. She captivated my attention with her tongue ring and two missing teeth. But beyond the surface and her profanity, I must admit the lesson I learned from her was invaluable. In what appeared to be a tirade about students bothering Sam, I learned a lesson. She said Sam never bothered students who didn't bother him, and she presented a history of Sam being misunderstood by teachers starting in kindergarten. She told me stories of how teachers had never bothered to pull his file to learn what his disability really is. None of the other teachers had known how to handle an autistic child. I silently listened and learned. She then called Sam out of art class and we talked to him together. She demonstrated for me how she speaks to him and disciplines him in an effective manner. From that day forward I never had severe issues with Sam. The conversation the three of us shared bonded us in a way that has changed our dynamics. Sam's mother knew that I would listen and respect her voice as a parent.

Think about it.

Why is it important to know the background of your students? Has there ever been a time when you did not want to know about your students' backgrounds?

_____

_____

_____

_____

_____

_____

_____

_____

_____

_____

_____

_____

_____

_____

_____

The scenario explained:

The teacher never took the time to investigate the true details of Sam's condition. She assumed she knew the right techniques to deal with his disability. The teacher's bias about children with disabilities was that they are all the same. She attempted to treat Sam as she would any other child. The teacher also brought bias about the mother. The teacher and her colleague made a value judgment about the mother based on her physical appearance. The missing teeth and tongue ring led to a very biased view for the teacher. The teacher and her colleague were also biased by the mother's demeanor and foul language. The two teachers immediately discredited her. Only after the teacher looked beyond her bias could she obtain the useful information needed to work with Sam.

––––

Scenario #4

I remember a situation that absolutely shocked me. I was helping with the performing arts and there was a teacher who was very young. At that time a lot of the girls looked at me as an adult but still very young so they were very comfortable talking to me and saying things they wouldn't say to their teachers. The girls were young—I'm talking ninth grade, tenth grade—and they would talk to me about the lead performing arts teacher. Now the lead teacher looked like the type you would see on MTV; she was very thin, very vain. Much of what she

valued had to do with looks. She told a lot of the girls that they needed to go on diets. Now these girls were not out of shape. Many of them played volleyball and basketball. But they would tell me how this teacher would point out specific things on their bodies. I actually wanted to fight her! I was stunned that someone in a position of authority would say something like that to a teenage girl. We already know that the teenage girl is extremely self-conscience from what she sees on TV and in magazines. Then she has someone in her every day life saying she thinks the girl is fat. Oh, and the student everyone knew was her favorite wore a size 1!!!!!

Think About it.

Have you ever had an experience where you witnessed a fellow co worker openly discriminate against students in anyway? If so what did you do? If not, what would you do if it were to happen?

_____

_____

_____

_____

_____

_____

_____

The scenario explained

Often times our colleagues need to have their discrimination pointed out to them. Many of the biases and prejudice harbored are subconscious or completely unconscious. It is our responsibility to make them aware of it for the sake of saving the students from the psychological damage that may result. In this situation the adult assisting this teacher should have had a professional and frank conversation about how obvious the prejudice was and how it negatively impacted the students. If a conversation of this nature does not prove effective, speak with an administrator.

———

Scenario #5

Mrs. Morris welcomed parents to her classroom at any time. She believed in having an open-door policy. One of her parents took that policy as a personal invitation to visit every day to inquire about her grandson's academic progress and classroom behavior. After getting a full report, which was also written in a behavior book on a daily basis, the grandmother would proceed to discipline or justify the student's inappropriate behavior. Well, on one particular afternoon when the teacher had decided that she did not feel like having a half-hour unscheduled conference with the determined woman, she proceeded out of the classroom toward the front office. Mrs. Morris's intent was to have the parent wrap up the conversation, so she could prepare materials for the next day and go home. Mrs. Grant, the student's grandmother, continued to analyze her grandson's behaviors all the way down the long, quiet hallway.

Mrs. Grant even followed Mrs. Morris into the front office. Once inside the office, Mrs. Morris quickly checked her mailbox and spoke briefly to the secretary about a phone message. The secretary informed her about a change in how one of her students would be going home each day. The student would be attending the after-school care program. Mrs. Grant asked, "What's the Kids Corner?" The secretary abruptly responded, "That's for working parents." The conservatively dressed woman replied sharply, "Excuse me!" The secretary stated again, "That's a program for working parents." Mrs. Morris was shocked and offended too. She couldn't believe that this older Asian woman made such ignorant comments to a woman, especially a black woman.

Mrs. Morris quickly interrupted the conversation and tried to convince the grandparent that Kids Corner was an after-school and before-school program that was available for families at the school. The parent was obviously irritated with the woman but she listened to what Mrs. Morris had to say. Then, she said sarcastically, "Thank you, Mrs. Morris, but I want her to know that I have my own business that I run out of my home!" The air was thick; however, Mrs. Morris was able to clear the air a bit when she discussed some of the activities that the after-school program provided for students who attended it. The secretary finally changed her tone and began commenting on the various programs

in the area provided for students in the evening. Despite the secretary's rudeness, Mrs. Grant remained poised and polite.

Think About it.

What mistake did the secretary make? Is there anything that the teacher could have done in this uncomfortable situation? Provide steps for de-escalating a situation such as this.

_____

_____

_____

_____

_____

_____

_____

_____

The scenario explained:

In this scenario the secretary demonstrated her biases toward the grandparent when she responded to her question about the after-school/before-school care program. She assumed that this mature, black/African-American woman was not working. She implied that she was not in need of the services provided by the program at the school. School staff members must never make assumptions about children and their parents. That means we must not make decisions for our parents based on what we think about our families based on what we may think about their race, finances, and/or abilities. When we display our biases we will offend others and they no longer respect us. In fact, other people will be discouraged from dealing with you. Those you offended will no longer want to interact with you because they will not view you as being a fair individual.

Conclusion

The goal of every individual who works in education or a mentoring program should be to enhance the lives of children and families. Many researchers have proven that there are numerous biases that cause us to negatively affect the lives of the people we interact with on a daily basis. Researcher Chris Bachrach from the staff of the National Institute of Child Health and Human Development (NICHD) explained bias with the following definition: bent, tendency, an inclination of temperament or outlook; especially: a personal and sometimes unreasoned judgment; prejudice; and instance of such prejudice. During a NICHD-sponsored workshop Bachrach emphasized during the introduction that "it is important to understand and acknowledge values underlying research and how values might influence the outcome" of research.(2001) This statement also has proven to be true in each of the cases or scenarios described in this section of the book. Although the focus of the workshop mentioned above was to address biases in intervention research it applies in many other areas. For example, Dr. Elizabeth Nowicki gives a more detailed overview of a study that examined "students' attitudes towards other students who may have different academic abilities or different ethnic backgrounds." In her recent publication, she concludes that the prejudices are impacted by the children's experience with having to

comment and assess their peers' abilities, ethnicity, and attitude components (Norwicki, 2008). In conclusion, each of the adults in these scenarios demonstrated biases that they developed from their own individual experiences.

Strategies and Tips

The following strategies have proven powerful when interacting with youth; we have found exceptional success with these when working with African American males:

1. Never have a fear factor.
2. Approach with a clean slate: Do not take into consideration any preexisting information and/or situations.
3. Approach as a mentorship: Set boundaries early so you will not have to be impacted by inappropriate actions.
4. Concentrate on what they can do and not what society says they can't do.
5. Have very realistic expectations.
6. Develop and train people who truly have a desire and passion to educate, mentor, and assist youth in reaching their full potential.
7. Many kids do like to be pushed.
8. Understand your role as the adult and leader of the classroom (I've learned that I am the adult and I will eventually prevail and get exactly what I want.)
9. In handling challenging behaviors, you must:

   a. Wait it out
   b. Be Patient
   c. Be Courteous
   d. Never be Afraid

10. Hold girls and boys to the same high standards in science and math.

11. Select boys and girls an equal number of times during a lesson.

12. Use inquiry-based activities that include manipulatives or hands-on materials in instructional lessons.

13. Encourage and provide assistance to all students.

14. Display images and reference areas in which contributions have been made by both genders.

15. Have students work in cooperative learning groups.

16. Monitor your voice, body language and attitude when you are interacting with students.

Research and experience have proven that the following strategies work when teachers are interacting with students:

- Don't put girls down or speak to them in a degrading manner.
- Don't force your anxieties about topics or skills, specifically in math and science, on students.
- Don't discourage students from asking questions about concepts by implying that they already know the answers.

Final Thoughts:

Experiences shape our belief and our beliefs define our actions.

Dr. Carter G. Woodson's *The Miseducation of the Negro* was published in 1933 during a time of forced racial segregation and Jim Crow laws. Dr. Woodson's seven decades of work should not mirror today's trials and tribulations but it does. As we read this powerful work, we were often taken back of how Dr. Woodson's words and observations.

The root we found were the educational impacts we had in our childhoods. Whether these educational impacts were from our family members or educators we were greatly affected. It forced each of us to tell our stories. It was a painful experience for some of us. At times the sharing felt like an unhealed wound but it was necessary to share so that the wound would heal. As you read our stories; think about your childhood educational experiences and how these experiences impact you in your role as teacher, counselor, administrator, parent, etc.

In the beginning you might have found our book to be confrontational because it challenges you to view yourself, challenge your behavior, and challenge your ideas when you are involved with children. You have also been enlightened by our own personal inhibitions that helped us to develop these phenomenal strategies and tips. By challenging you to develop your own personal story, we believe we can help you understand why what you were doing was ineffective and frustrating for all concerned. We strongly recommend that when you begin applying your knowledge, you will get the results you desire: SUCCESS.

Our experiences and beliefs are real. Our interactions and relationships with today's youths must be based on realness. To be real—in this context—means to acknowledge the strengths and weaknesses of who we are so that we can successfully acknowledge the strengths and weaknesses of the youth we are charged to develop. Because of the challenges you have faced or continuing facing, you will find yourself to be more likely to follow a structure change by using the strategies and tips that we outlined.

If we want to motivate today's youths to be the best they can be we must be the best. We become the best by sharing strategies and tips that worked for us and revealing the things that did not work for us. We must read and attend classes and conferences on subjects that focus on our youths. We must not be afraid to say we need help and be willing to accept that help no matter what our experience level is. And always remember in working with children that you are the most important tool they have. Your healthy mind, body, and spirit are the first, last, and most important requirements for success in your job.

This is a start of a movement. A movement of bold African-American educators willing to say what needs to be said and do what needs to be done so that our students will see and act on their greatness.

www.ingramcontent.com/pod-product-compliance
Lightning Source LLC
Chambersburg PA
CBHW060132050426
42448CB00010B/2084

Secret Love or; The Maiden Queen by John Dryden

A Tragi-comedy

John Dryden was born on August 9th, 1631 in the village rectory of Aldwincle near Thrapston in Northamptonshire. As a boy Dryden lived in the nearby village of Titchmarsh, Northamptonshire. In 1644 he was sent to Westminster School as a King's Scholar.

Dryden obtained his BA in 1654, graduating top of the list for Trinity College, Cambridge that year.

Returning to London during The Protectorate, Dryden now obtained work with Cromwell's Secretary of State, John Thurloe.

At Cromwell's funeral on 23 November 1658 Dryden was in the company of the Puritan poets John Milton and Andrew Marvell. The setting was to be a sea change in English history. From Republic to Monarchy and from one set of lauded poets to what would soon become the Age of Dryden.

The start began later that year when Dryden published the first of his great poems, Heroic Stanzas (1658), a eulogy on Cromwell's death.

With the Restoration of the Monarchy in 1660 Dryden celebrated in verse with Astraea Redux, an authentic royalist panegyric.

With the re-opening of the theatres after the Puritan ban, Dryden began to also write plays. His first play, The Wild Gallant, appeared in 1663 but was not successful. From 1668 on he was contracted to produce three plays a year for the King's Company, in which he became a shareholder. During the 1660s and '70s, theatrical writing was his main source of income.

In 1667, he published Annus Mirabilis, a lengthy historical poem which described the English defeat of the Dutch naval fleet and the Great Fire of London in 1666. It established him as the pre-eminent poet of his generation, and was crucial in his attaining the posts of Poet Laureate (1668) and then historiographer royal (1670).

This was truly the Age of Dryden, he was the foremost English Literary figure in Poetry, Plays, translations and other forms.

In 1694 he began work on what would be his most ambitious and defining work as translator, The Works of Virgil (1697), which was published by subscription. It was a national event.

John Dryden died on May 12th, 1700, and was initially buried in St. Anne's cemetery in Soho, before being exhumed and reburied in Westminster Abbey ten days later.

Index of Contents

PREFACE AND PROLOGUE

The Maiden Queen is said, by Langbaine, to be founded upon certain passages in "The Grand Cyrus," and in "Ibrahim, the illustrious Bassa." Few readers will probably take the trouble of consulting these huge volumes, for the purpose of ascertaining the truth of this charge. Even our duty, as editors, cannot impel us to the task; satisfied, as we are, that, since these ponderous folios at that time loaded every toilette, Dryden can hardly have taken more from such well-known sources, than the mere outline of the story. Indeed, to a certain degree, the foundation of the plot, upon a story in the "Cyrus," is admitted by the author. The character of the queen is admirably drawn, and the catastrophe is brought very artfully forward; the uncertainty, as to her final decision, continuing till the last moment. In this, as in all our author's plays, some passages of beautiful poetry occur in the dialogue; as, for example, the scene in act 3d betwixt Philocles and Candiope. The characters, excepting that of the Maiden Queen herself, are lame and uninteresting. Philocles, in particular, has neither enough of love to make him despise ambition, nor enough of ambition to make him break the fetters of love. We might have admired him, had he been constant; or sympathised with him, had he sinned against his affections, and repented; but there is nothing interesting in the vacillations of his indecision. The comic part of the play contains much of what was thought wit in the reign of Charles II.; for marriage is railed against, and a male and female rake join in extolling the pleasures of a single life, even while the usage of the theatre compels them, at length, to put on the matrimonial chains. It is surprising, that no venturous author, in that gay age, concluded, by making such a couple happy in their own way. The novelty of such a catastrophe would have insured its success; and, unlike to the termination of the loves of Celadon and Florimel, it would have been strictly in character.

The Maiden Queen was first acted in 1667; and printed, as the poet has informed us, by the command of Charles himself, who graced it with the title of HIS play. Dryden mentions the excellence of the acting, so it was probably received very favourably.